HELPERS
OF
DESTINY

Leveraging People God brings into your Life to Fulfil Your Destiny

By

AYO OLULEYE

Copyright © 2020 by Ayo Oluleye

All rights reserved. No part of this book may be reproduced or used in any manner without written permission of the copyright owner except for the use of quotations in a book review.

FIRST EDITION

Paperback: 978-1-80227-348-9
eBook: 978-1-80227-349-6

facebook.com/ayorinde.Oluleye/

Published by PublishingPush.com

THANSKSGIVING AND DEDICATION

I thank God for His Mercy and Favour upon me. He is my chief helper of destiny, without Him I am nothing, but with God, I am all things He wants me to be. I also thank God for enabling me put my thoughts about Helpers of Destiny into a book that will be a blessing to many.

This book is dedicated to my beautiful wife and the two wonderful Children God has given to us as gifts

I want to appreciate my dear wife Nkechi, my queen and jewel, that God has given me as my help mate. She has been with me through thick and thin, the good and challenging times. Thank you for your support in making the publication of this book a reality.

To my children Prince Oluwasegun and Princess Shalom, I love and appreciate you for your understanding, especially when you had to make sacrifices for my sake that allowed me settle down to write this book.

PREFACE

The inspiration to write this book came as I observed people struggling through life, not feeling fulfilled and having next to nothing in terms of accomplishment. I discovered that many are not feeling fulfilled in life because the help they need, especially from people, is not forth-coming.

God has created every human being for a particular purpose and to carry out an assignment here on Earth. This can be described as destiny. I believe every resource, including the human resources required to fulfil our destiny is right here on earth. To fulfil our destiny, we need other people to assist us. This book explores how God has created human beings with the capacity to help one another to fulfil their purpose. We are all interdependent. The importance of human connectivity is aptly put by the wise words of Martin Luther King Jr, **"Whatever affects one directly, affects all indirectly. I can never be what I ought to be until you are what you ought to be and you can never be what you ought to be until I am what I ought to be. This is the interrelated structure of reality."**

I hope this book will help us see every person as a gift from God, created with the capacity to help another person. Asking for help from another person does not undermine our self-worth. We all need some form of help from somebody to accomplish anything worthwhile in life.

I agree with the comments of the unknown author who said we should, "Be strong enough to stand alone, smart enough to know when we need help, and brave enough to ask for it."

Our destiny being fulfilled is not only in our hands, but also in the hands of people who God has raised to help us. I call them **"HELPERS OF DESTINY"**.

This book has been written from a Christian perspective, but I believe non-Christians will be able to relate to the life issues raised in the book.

I want to thank Ajigbotoluwa Oluwatosin for the excellent typesetting of this book and also appreciate William McMahon for the editing and Diane Newton for the superb proof reading of the manuscript

Read this book with an open mind; and it will indeed transform and bless you.

COMMENTARY

The book, **'Helpers of Destiny'** is not just another literature, it is a careful and diligent dissection of secrets to success, a revelation of the principles for productive and profitable life as well as a diagnosis and discovery of the reasons for living. The Helpers of Destiny can simply be summed up as giving is living.

In this book, Bro Ayo is calling our attention to the essence of co-existence, and the fact that we need one another. Just as no single-gender can produce a baby without the collaboration of the opposite sex, no child can give birth to him/herself without the effort of a woman, and no one can bury him/herself at death without the help of the living; so, it is that no one born of a woman can realize his/ her reason for existence, maximize the life and fulfil destiny without the help of other people.

Destiny is like a building; the quality of help and quantity of resources a house receives determines the magnificence of it or lack of it. The quality of help and quantity of resources a man receives from others determine how great or how little that man will become in life.

I hope that many people will read this book, and be inspired to begin to appreciate the gift of lives around them.

—**Pastor Solomon Bamidele**
Senior Pastor of Dominion Gospel Church Thornton Heath
London United Kingdom

Contents

Thansksgiving and Dedication iii

Preface iv

Commentary vi

Introduction 8

Chapter One: The Power of Relationship 12

Chapter Two: Trust in God At All Times 21

Chapter Three: Help from Unexpected Quarters 27

Chapter Four: Well-Positioned for Help 35

Chapter Five: Never Despise Your Helpers of Destiny 39

Chapter Six: Your Pushers in Life 45

Chapter Seven: Beware of Destiny Killers 56

Chapter Eight: Where Do You Need Help? 75

Chapter Nine: Reality of the Help of Others 79

Prayer Points 83

INTRODUCTION

> *"If you're not making someone else's life better, then you're wasting your time. Your life will become better by making other lives better."*
>
> —Will Smith

Human beings are an everlasting conundrum. We are the only beings God created with such a complex and layered consciousness, and to cope with the realization of what it means to be human, God designed us as the ultimate social being, created with the capacity to interact and bond with fellow human beings. We cannot claim to be an island *wholly* unto ourselves. We may experience our own birth and death individually, but God has created human beings to complement one another during life. No single human being has all the answers to the challenges his or her life may present. God, as well as a personal faith with this greater significance, is the purest pathway to explore and discover the answers to all of life's most pressing existential questions. God has never made any human being to exist alone without a helper.

In the most fundamental Biblical example, God gave the Male Man the walled paradisical Garden of Eden to cultivate. He also gave Man dominion over everything in the walled garden; but God in His wisdom knew Man would be a ruinous mess without a helper.

> *"And the Lord God said it is not good that the man should be alone. I will make him a help meet for him."*
>
> **—Genesis 2: 18 KJV**

Within the context of scripture, God created Female woman for the Male man to assist him; but looking at the bigger picture, this "coupling" arrangement by God is a model for many human relationships. Everyone needs a helper in one form or the other.

We have all been created for a divine purpose. No one is an accident or a waste. We are embodied with a miraculous value worthy of further exploration. The divine purpose for which you were created is called your 'DESTINY'. To fulfil that purpose (Destiny), we need a relationship with God.

We must realise, however, that God sent forth divine help for "Man" in the form of "Man" himself: our Lord Jesus Christ. Jesus came down to provide navigation in solving the problems of humanity, revealing the origin of sin and his chosen eternal destiny. Our Lord even had to select 12 disciples to help with His assignment on Earth. If our Lord Jesus Christ employed helping hands for His ministry here on earth, we should take the easy cue and bond together in an endeavour to fulfil our destinies. God has placed some of the things we need to accomplish our divine assignment in the hands of people with what could be conceptualized as "divine gifts" bestowed to them. It is our duty to identify these "chosen" people and connect to them in forging a stronger individual – and whole of humanity.

God wants us to fulfil our destiny in life and walk through the centre of our purpose on Earth. We must, however, remember that we cannot do it alone. God calls us alone in our dreams but does not expect us to "go" it alone in reality. We need to be surrounded by people who believe in what we are called to do – those who are ready to help us fulfil our calling. I call these people, **'HELPERS OF DESTINY'.** These are people God has assigned to our life to help us fulfil our divine assignment here on earth.

The status of the person in relation to us does not determine who will be our helpers in life. They may be rich or poor, old or young, bright or less - it doesn't matter. Educated or not, employee or employer, master or servant, it makes no difference.

Also remember that in heaven, God doesn't walk around asking, "I'm sorry, what was your ethnicity?" So racial and ethnic undertones should not influence who you determine your divine-sent help to be. The position or place in life of our helper of destiny is indeed designed to be unpredictable. Take the story of Naaman in the Bible; he could never have imagined that the slave girl in his house was the one that would lead to his healing. This seemingly insignificant Hebrew slave girl was, by our definitions, a "helper of destiny" in the life of Naaman.

No human-being should be under-estimated. The person we look down upon may be the person God brought into our life to help fulfil our destiny. This simple reason informs us why we should not malign or despise the people God has brought into our life. Every relationship with anyone is a divine opportunity to sow a seed that will produce either a good fruit or a bad fruit. It is up to us to sow the right kind of seed in people we come into contact with, so as to reap the good fruit in future.

CHAPTER ONE

THE POWER OF RELATIONSHIP

> *"Each relationship nurtures a strength or weakness within you."*
>
> —Mike Murdoch

The totality of our life is summarised in the meshwork of our relationships. At its core, these include relationships with God, yourself, and with one another. Before you can begin having solid, fruitful, sustainable relationships with others, look inward to resolve your relationship with the inner kingdom first.

The impact of your good relationship with God rubs off on how you relate to your surroundings, whether it be a loving and positive manner or something less desirable. If you have no personal self-worth, it becomes difficult to have a positive and healthy relationship with other people. You cannot offer what you do not have, so make sure you have a solid foundation before you go trying to make the lives of others better. The Scripture says Love your neighbour as you love yourself (Matthew 22:39 GNB). You can only love one another when you love yourself. If you hate or despise who you are, then you are not capable of either loving another, or having a positive and effective relationship with other people.

I was reminded of the power of these communal bonds by a story about clashing citizens of East and West Germany during the Cold War. One day, suffering from their authoritarian rule, the East Germans decided to dump their trash and garbage over the Berlin Wall, into West Germany. The West Germans could have responded in kind justifiably, but they took the route of higher order. Stoically and powerfully, The West Germans took a truck load of canned goods, bread, milk and other provisions, and neatly stacked it on the East Berlin side. On top of this stack, they placed the sign: "EACH GIVES WHAT HE HAS".

How very true! You can only give what you have. A person with hate inside of them cannot give love. A person that inhabits violence can never give peace. If a person has evil inside of them, they can never give good. Learn to generate these feelings through your inner strength and the wisdom born from your relationship with God.

At every stage and moment of our life, we meet different people who we form all kinds of relationships with. I will categorise relationships into three broad categories to simplify the discussion: short, medium, and long-term relationships.

A short-term relationship is a kind of relationship we have for a passing moment. This kind of relationship is not normally a close relationship: for example, the bus driver that we come in contact with on the bus; the bank clerk on the counter in the bank; the sales assistant we met in the shop; the interviewer we met at the job application interview. Though we met these people for a brief moment, they could be of tremendous impact upon our life so as to affect our destiny for good or evil. Do not underestimate the summative power of all the little engagements and "short-term" relationships you cultivate every day as you walk through the world. Philip came into the life of the Ethiopian eunuch on one occasion. That singular brief encounter did not only transform the Ethiopian Eunuch, but it also brought the gospel to Africa - Acts 8: 26-39 KJV.

A medium-term relationship is a relationship for a more certain duration of time. It is not for a moment of just "passing or ferrying" through. Some close relationships fall under this category. The relationship with a teacher in school is one such relationship. Relations with co-workers in the workplace is a medium-term relationship. Be aware that medium-term relationships, as described here, can be cultivated into long-term relationships. However, do not underestimate the enduring love and consistent shows of support it takes to achieve these transformational relationships. It takes real enduring effort and an almost-uncomfortable self-awareness.

The deepest of any relationship, a long-term relationship, is what can be described as a life-time relationship; it is a very bonded and close relationship: for example, the relationship between parents and children or husband and wife. Blood relations generally fall within this category, too. There is a blood bond in this relationship, which makes it stronger and more intimate. This kind of relationship should not be treated with levity. It is not everyone we have such a relationship with who will be supportive of our destiny, but we are stuck with them by a blood bond. That does not mean they cannot hurt you; simply recognize their uncanny similarities and differences to your life path.

Within these different categories of relationships, God has positioned people who will assist us in fulfilling our destiny. It is important that we do not take any relationship for granted. We do so at our own peril. The test of the value you place on a person is determined by how you relate with them.

Every human being is created by God, and naturally has a self-worth and inherent dignity attached to them. It is inappropriate to exercise authority in disdain or meaningless domination of others. No one is called just to degrade and dominate another person. Leadership is not about domination. That is why Christian countries like America have moved toward democracy. Dictatorships must be opposed in any form; they strip so many people of respectful and honourable treatment.

A CEO should not wield their power at liberty in efforts to victimise or suppress their subordinates. The subordinate will also do well not to undermine the authority of their boss. No position of leadership should be abused.

The truth is, whoever comes to help or serve us is God's gift. We must honour and respect God's gift. My belief is that everyone is called to serve and help another. A person who is not interested in helping and serving others can never fulfil their own destiny. The more we help and serve others, the more chances we may get of people coming our way to help and serve us. Just keep that fact in mind next time someone asks for a simple favour; a simple accommodation could lead to a lifetime of fruitful gratitude.

The people that God has brought into our life in whatever capacity are there to help us fulfil our purpose. Depending on what is done or not in the relationship, it may make or ruin phases of our life. Life moves in a circle, just as the world does: it goes around. The servant today may be the master tomorrow.

Our attitude towards people is largely a matter of choice. We choose how to engage and respond to the world around us, and it is up to us to make sense of how we fit into the bigger picture. Just remember, there are consequences to the choices we make. Whatever a person sows, they will reap. Are we sowing seeds that add value to a life, or devalue a life?

The journey of life no doubt causes us to meet a lot of people within what is now a global network. God uses the people He brings into our life as a means to achieve our destiny. God allows different sorts of people to come into our life: The Good and The Bad; The Gentle and The Harsh; The Patient and The Impatient; The Rich and The Poor; The Wise and The Foolish and so on. These different types of people have come our way to perform one role or another in the fulfilment of our destiny. **Never say that you regret having a relationship, even if it was a sour one**. The Lord always permits a relationship for a purpose; and it is our duty to discover the purpose of any relationship to enable us to reap the benefit. If nothing else at all, there is a lesson to be learnt from every relationship.

When we properly examine every person who has come into our life, we will see the multitude of ways they have impacted our life and destiny in one way or another. Relationships present the chance for advancement in the eyes of God. He wants to test our consciousness and see how we respond to a world of our own making.

Strangely, even in a relationship that has caused us harm, there is an inherent opportunity to achieve greatness. Think of the story of Joseph in the Old Testament – his brothers thought they had buried his destiny by selling him into slavery. Neither they, nor Joseph, knew that their actions would push Joseph into the Land vital for fulfilling his destiny. God can always bring good out of the evil people intended against us. Turn their dirt to soil, and you bloom up out of it. Let us always seek to find the good out of every relationship we are involved in.

As I said earlier, the people, God brings into our life are gifts. God's gifts are meant to empower and align us with our destiny. It is important that we build healthy and strong relationships that support our destiny.

The people we surround ourselves with play a factor as to whether we will be a success or a failure. Who you chose as your spouse determines whether your marital life succeeds or fails; the business partner you choose may make or mar your business; the people you choose to employ may grow or destroy your establishment; the workers you select to run a project drive its success or failure, etc. Be open to changes if you get a gut feeling that someone is entrenching themselves in a potentially ruinous situation around you.

The bedrock of any sustainable relationship is communication, trust, mutual respect, integrity and loyalty. Always remember this. Write it down in a journal now to commit these tenets to your heart and memory.

Communication is one of the most important keys to a relationship that will last; it is like oxygen to life - without it, it dies. I know we can talk about all kinds of communication to express ourselves, but it is essential that whatever way we communicate, it must be open, with people having a firm internal grasp of what is being expressed. It is advisable to check each other's understanding to avoid misinterpretation of what was communicated. A build-up of even slight miscommunications may seriously strain a relationship. To receive the appropriate help, it is important that we convey our thoughts, points and feelings effectively to those who could help us.

A relationship devoid of trust is hypocritical and will never be healthy. These relationships are purely transactional until someone catches the betrayal "hot potato." Commitment is impossible where there is no trust - it inhibits the readiness to support each other because of ulterior motives drawing our attention away.

Respect must be reciprocal if a relationship is to yield a positive outcome that will be beneficial to the parties. When there is mutual respect, there is an appreciation of the individual differences; sensitivity to people's feelings; and identifying with each other's needs.

There is a popular saying stating, "integrity is everything". Matthew 5:37 NKJV supports this assertion: "But let your 'Yes' be 'Yes', and your 'No', 'No'. For whatever is more than these is from the evil one." A relationship based on integrity waxes stronger and stronger, can withstand any storm, and operates from the angle of sincerity, which is quite helpful to people in a relationship.

Loyalty is commitment, devotion, faithfulness. Loyalty must be mutual for it to produce a positive result. Some demand loyalty from people, but do not intend to give loyalty back. A one-sided loyalty is an abusive relationship; for example, a man who wants his wife to be faithful, but is not faithful himself, or a leader who wants his followers to be loyal to him but betrays them for his own selfish interest. You cannot be disloyal to people and expect loyalty from them. The world will punish you severely for such foolish beliefs.

It must be said that we cannot be in a close relationship with every person we come in contact with. We can choose certain relationships, but we cannot choose all. The bottom line is whatever the relationship, endeavour to relate in peace and love with everyone. Don't make the prejudgement that you know the role any person is meant to play in your life, for the answer may surprise you.

God sometimes allow us to have relationships with difficult people to prune us, to knock off our ego that we may be a testimony for Jesus Christ. The importance of light is only appreciated in the midst of darkness. Christians are called to be light in the world of darkness and salt in the world of bitterness.

God has called Christians specially to influence the world around them positively; and the only way this will happen is when they relate with the people in the world. Jesus said, "He is the friend of sinners." He is not the friend of their sins, but the friend of the person who commits the sin. As ambassadors for Christ, we must be friends of sinners but not their sins. Over time learn to befriend your enemies, to influence them in a positive manner and present the gospel of the Kingdom of God to them so they can receive salvation.

CHAPTER TWO

TRUST IN GOD AT ALL TIMES

> *"It is better to trust in the Lord than to put confidence in man. It is better to trust in the Lord than to put confidence in princes."*
>
> —Psalms 118: 8-9

It is important to state at this chapter that our ultimate helper and anchor of our destiny is God; and we must avoid putting blind trust in the people around us. They are fallible, as are we, but the God in us as Christians is an enduring source of divine wisdom and advancement. As much as we are to honour and respect people, no human being should take the place of God in our life. That will amount to idolatry, something tragically common within authoritarian states. In countries like North Korea, the political leaders "hijack" Biblical myths, making themselves false idols while shamelessly abusing their people. Take these extreme examples in the real world as the costs of false idolatry. Never put a human above the sovereignty and omniscience of the Almighty God.

> *"I will lift up my eyes to the hills. From whence comes my help? My help comes from the Lord, Who made Heaven and Earth."*
>
> **—Psalm 121:1-2 NKJV**

Our trust must always be in God, who is the helper that never fails. A Helper of your Destiny is only a vessel through whom God has decided to assist and help you. God is sovereign in all things; and He is the link to the Helper of Destiny. God should not be neglected in the favour of the Helper of your Destiny. Do not anoint a human being as seer of your life.

Human beings in their natural state can act aggressively, selfishly and ignorantly. At times, it can seem we rarely want to help another, or at the very least make it easier on each other. God is the superior personality who urges or influences people to help – a connectedness to a feeling of righteousness that is hard to fully abstract.

When we remove our focus from God and concentrate on Man, we risk cutting off the link – the spark - that empowers us to connect us to man. It is God that worketh in people both to will and do His righteous pleasure. Always make God the main focus and not men of flesh. We should remain connected to God so that the bridge linking us to our Destiny Helper is not removed. God is our main source of life and **Ultimate Helper of Destiny. He is the energy source, the bridge between us – He is the source of the very air that breathes us into being.**

For he hath said, I will never leave thee, nor forsake thee. So that we may boldly say The Lord is my helper, and I will not fear what man shall do unto me".

—Hebrew 13: 5c-6

We can do without a person if we must. However, we cannot do without a relationship with God and the kingdom of God within us. Otherwise, not only do we lose our direction; we lose the compass itself.

When God puts people in a position to help us, and they refuse, God will raise other people on our behalf. No human being is indispensable in God's eyes. It is a divine privilege to be of assistance and aid to another. The helper should not abuse the privilege by manipulating or making unnecessary demands from the recipient of the help. The world works in mysterious ways, and do not try to play God by pulling strings through this high-level, yet simply selfish, deception.

By helping another, we are indeed fulfilling our divine assignment (Destiny). I would further say that we should see the person we are helping as our helper of destiny. If we had not met the recipient of the help, we would not have been operating around our central purpose in life. We answer divine calls when we help another, and we prepare the ground for God's blessings in our life.

"What you make happen to others, God will make happen for you"

—Mike Murdock.

We remember in the Bible, the story of Esther, a slave girl who became a Queen in a foreign Land, against all odds. Her Uncle Mordecai sent a message to her that she needed to go before the King to avert the calamity that was about to befall the Jewish race at the instigation of Haman - the tyrannical enemy of the Jews. This was a hard demand to act on because as a Persian Queen, it was illegal for Esther to go before the King if she had not been called. At first, Esther wrote back that she was helpless to gain audience with the King in favour of the Jews.

In response, Mordecai wrote that as a Jew, Esther would perish at the hands of Haman's genocidal intent either way. However, as a Jewish Queen in Persia, it was more likely that God raised her there to aid the Chosen People, and another would rise if she did not fulfil her duties as Queen. This convinced Esther to gracefully invite the King to two dinners before, at a crucial moment, revealing Haman's bloody plans to raze Jewish lands to the ground. The king, having been charmed by Esther's wonderful presentation, sprang to her defence.

It seems that Mordecai understood God must have allowed Esther, an insignificant Jewish slave girl, to become a Queen in a foreign land for this particular purpose. In their moment of need she rose up and carried out the will of her God in the most spectacular way. God linked Esther and Mordecai together, according to the Biblical text, through Himself; it is a beautiful divine ideal to behold.

Whatever the position of authority we occupy, God has placed us there for a particular purpose that manifests itself as legitimate and enduring benefit to others.

Many are disappointed and distressed when someone they expect to perform as a godly idol fails to follow through on their "too good to be true" promises. Here, the grief stems from putting their trust in a person of flesh rather than the omniscience of God. The Bible says we operate under a curse when we put our trust in a human being. It must be understood that human beings are limited by their thoughts and bound by their flesh. A person may have it in mind to help, but what if circumstances beyond their control make it impossible to give what they intended or promised? You can plan a pretty picnic as a human being, but you cannot predict the weather. You'd do best to remember that when considering the role of God in your life.

Many have put their expectation on one uncle, aunt, friend or close relation somewhere in a position of authority to help them. Many have forged strong bonds, but even blood family relatives can leave us disappointed. We must realise that nobody can help us, no matter how close they are to us, unless God has ordained them to be our helper of destiny.

The way of God is quite different from our ways. As the Heaven is far away from the Earth, so is the way of God far away from our ways. God reserves the prerogative of who He is going to assign to help us to fulfil our destiny. Help, more often than not, generates from unexpected places.

This phenomenon gives insight into how there must be a higher-order power that is sovereign, apparently doing what He pleases through whatever vessel of His choosing. God uses the weak things of this world to confound the strong, and foolish things to confound the wise.

A follower of Jesus from the Bible named Nathanael said, "Can anything good come out of Nazareth?" The people of Nazareth were regarded as a people of a low status in Israel, and more or less like the outcasts in society. God in His Sovereignty decided that our Lord Jesus Christ would live in Nazareth, and come out of Nazareth. This is why in some places in the Bible, we see Jesus described as Jesus Christ of Nazareth. From the rejected corners of society, God brought out the manifestation of holiness on Earth, The King of kings through whom the whole world would receive salvation.

I will be talking more about help from unexpected quarters in the next chapter.

CHAPTER THREE

HELP FROM UNEXPECTED QUARTERS

> *"Many are the strange chances of the world,' said Mithrandir, 'and help oft shall come from the hands of the weak when the Wise falter."*
>
> —JRR Tolkien

My senior sister related to me an experience she had with her cousin-in-law's wife, where the woman was very hostile for some unknown reason, during a visit to the cousin-law's house. She gave my sister a spiteful look and did her best to make it clear that she was not welcome. She refused to respond to my sister's greeting, creating even more tension. For some strange reason the attitude of the woman did not provoke anger in my sister for the duration of the visit.

Regardless, my sister's husband noticed the attitude of his cousin's wife and raised it with my sister. He asked her what could have warranted such a combative posture from this woman. My sister could not understand, as she had no prior misunderstanding with her. It seemed the two would never get along or be able to see eye-to-eye on successful endeavours.

God had other plans in mind; several months after the incident, the same woman who had humiliated her during that family get-together introduced her to big clients in a bid to benefit her food catering business. My sister said she made a lot of money from the introduction, and legitimate fruit bore from my senior sister not lashing out due to the misunderstanding. Staying calm and enduring the confusing behaviour gave her cousin-in-law's wife the right space and frame of mind to become "help from unexpected quarters." My sister never, *ever* thought help would come from this woman, especially when considering their tense family exchanges.

Help does not normally come from places and people we expect. It is important that we are open minded and do not rule out people as capable of helping us. These preconceived notions and ideas hold us back every day. Honour and celebrate every relationship, and look for ways to help the bond bear more fruit in the eyes of God.

There is an African Proverb which says," Human beings are like a river that the waters flow to unimaginable destinations." Never look down on any human being; God may use our arch enemy to help us. In the Book of Esther, we can relate to the story of how Haman, Mordecai's arch enemy, was used to elevate and bestow honour upon him. See Esther 6: 1-11 KJV

The following verse in the Bible -1 Corinthians 1:27-29 KJV is very instructive on the point that the ways of God are not the ways of man.

> *"But God hath chosen the foolish things of the world to confound the wise; and God hath chosen the weak things of the world to confound the things which are mighty; and the base things of the world, and the things which are despised hath God chosen, Yea and things which are not, to bring to nought things that are; That no flesh should glory in his presence."*
>
> **—1 Corinthians 1:27-29 KJV**

Being alert, vigilant and watchful is an important trait required to be able to spot our helper of destiny. Identifying our helper of destiny may sometimes require moving from where we are to a relative place where we can better see who our helper of destiny is. We need to be flexible, adaptable to change, and move out of our comfort zone to get acquainted with our helper of destiny. To move out of our comfort zone can be painful, but the sacrifice is worth it. Finding ways to lean into these moments of "un-comfortability" is an art that helps us, as people, to grow stronger over time.

For example, if the person God has assigned to help us is in a remote village in Africa, and it is the will of God that we move to the village, then we need to move to the village. Our failure to move to get connected to that person in the village in Africa will leave us static and unfulfilled - a hole that cannot be patched up until the voyage is made.

Divinely connecting to our helper of destiny sometimes requires taking a step of faith, which could appear contrary to common sense.

The story of Ruth in the Bible comes to mind. If Ruth had not left Moab and followed Naomi to Israel, she would not have met with Boaz, her helper of destiny. The action Ruth took to follow Naomi to Israel after her husband died made no sense. Naomi was a widow with no hope of bearing children. In Biblical times these "barren" women received unfair and unjustifiable treatment. To push back against these preconceived notions, Ruth had to make an extreme sacrifice, which was contrary to human logic; but God was guiding a higher purpose for Ruth and Naomi. God may be asking some of us to make such sacrifices before we can get connected to the helper God has prepared for us. We need to take a step of faith to get to the centre of God's plan for our life. Help, most times, comes from unexpected quarters.

The unexpected could come from unknown admirers. The words of encouragement and help they render is aid we would never ask for. They notice a skill or a talent in us, and when something comes up that relates to that skill or talent, they go out of their way to connect us to it.

Such was the case of King David. While he is now known as the symbol of power and pride for Jews around the world, there was a time when David was a lowly servant in King Saul's home.

In his later years, as his rule grew more erratic and tyrannical, members of Saul's court would have someone play the king an instrument. The music, incidentally, would calm his fits of rage. After seeing David playing the harp one day, a servant recommended David be the main actor to calm King Saul with his music; this servant brought David into the palace he would one day rule over, thus providing help from unexpected places. Who could have guessed this unknown admirer would help David's destiny in such a remarkable manner? - See 1 Samuel 16: 14- 23

We might be involved in one good deed in one remote place and think that we are unnoticed. God is very interested in what we do when no one else is looking, so who knows? One day that behaviour will carry over in public, organically generating more and more secret admirers of our good works. Whatever good we do, let us continue. What we regard as a hobby might be the springboard that will take us to our destiny land. There is an unknown admirer watching and ready to promote us wherever an opening occurs.

When connected to our helper, do not begin to try and prognosticate on how they are going to help us specifically. God has ordained and anointed our helper specially to help us; and the same God will direct our helper in the way and manner they will help us.

Many have missed it because they wanted to dictate to their helper the way they were to be helped. If we were in control of such infinite complexities there would be no need for God to send us a helper. Let us be humble, and submit to the seemingly inexplicable ways our helper pushes us toward our destiny.

Remember now the Biblical story of Naaman, an Army General suffering from a leprosy disease. The Prophet Elisha had instructed Naaman to go and dip himself into the River Jordan seven times and he would be healed of his leprosy. Naaman took offence and felt slighted, thinking that the man of God, Elisha, should have come out to meet him to pray and possibly lay hands on him. Naaman turned back in annoyance, disregarding the instructions of Elisha. Naaman later obeyed the instructions of Elisha at the urging of his servants and was cured of his leprosy. Naaman would have missed the healing because of his pride and presumption. Use all your faculties when deciding whether someone means you help or harm, but do not foolishly assume you know, right away, the value of a Destiny Helper's insight.

2 Kings 5: 10-14 KJV.

TESTIMONY OF MY DARLING WIFE

It all happened when my son gained admission into the university and was unable to get an accommodation on campus. He was put on the accommodation waiting list. We asked that he stayed in the bed and breakfast until the accommodation issue was sorted. After a long wait and spending a lot of money on the bed and breakfast accommodation, my son got frustrated and had to vent to us on the phone. Life was quickly turning out not how my son planned at university; he felt his dreams were being smothered by stupid housing issues. My boy was learning to hold the weight of the world on his shoulders, and I felt dearly for him.

I can never forget that Friday he called and said, "Mum, I am trying to hold back tears and am getting frustrated about the whole set up. The school is messing up my mind, I can't concentrate on my studies. If I come home, I will never go back to that University again."

I had to hold back my own tears because I know my son is a strong person emotionally, and rarely is he disturbed about situations. I had to encourage him, and told him to hold unto God; that God would come through for him. I knew nobody living in the university area. I was on the road when he called me. While it must have seemed like a meaningless exercise to those passing by in cars, I then stood by the roadside, and spoke to God and said, "God I have hosted people in my house in London, even strangers. Now Lord, my son is in a place where he has no relations, stranded. O Lord come raise help for my son."

I had now got to the place where I was to pick up cooking items, when suddenly I heard a voice telling me to ask the owner of the shop if he knew anyone staying in the town where my son's university was? Another voice, pretending to be smug and incredibly rational said, "Why would you do that? That makes no sense; I don't see the logical pattern or progression in it. This is stupid."

Fortunately, I have learnt to recognise when God speaks, and I decided to ask the shop owner as instructed by the Holy Spirit. To my delight, but no surprise, the shop owner said he had a friend in the town. He contacted the person by phone, and within 15 minutes, they agreed to host my son at a reasonable sum. The Holy Spirit is a great helper. Help from an unexpected place came and gave my son a place to rest his head after long days of studying. I could not have been more grateful - I asked and received from Him.

CHAPTER FOUR

WELL-POSITIONED FOR HELP

"Never be afraid to reach out for help when you are sinking. It may make a world of difference."

—Mikel Sanders

In the last chapter, I spoke about the story of Ruth in the Bible. The sacrifice she made by leaving Moab to come to Israel, and meeting with Boaz bears much significance. From this story, we see the importance of being well positioned for our helper to identify us – Ruth 2: 3-4

Ruth positioned herself in the sightline of Boaz out in the field such that Boaz was able to single out and identify her. If she had not been well positioned, Boaz may have never noticed the woman. We should not hide from the glare of our helper of destiny. Prepare intensively, so you can be seen and recognized by those who may have a gift or wisdom to offer you. Being at the right place at the right time involves prior preparation, and a hand of favour – conceivably provided by God.

Hang around the right people that can solve the problem you cannot solve, and be well-positioned for them to render the necessary help. Most people do not know the help they need. That is OK and actually a part of the entire process. Take it upon yourself to be proactive, letting people know what areas of your life you would like help in. In short, **your helpers of destiny will not come to you because you need them, but because you pursue them. You attract what and who you pursue, so embrace the human agency in finding your helper of destiny. It is a wonderful part of the journey when thoroughly explored.**

Being well positioned may involve building certain knowledge bases, skills and abilities. It might entail personal studies. For example, going to school for further training could be a path well-travelled for many; attending seminars and training courses can spark up a life's purpose; Retraining for another discipline and engaging in personal research through various credible sources are other powerful ways to position yourself well in the eyes of God - and your Helpers of Destiny.

Whatever price we must pay to be well positioned for aid is worth it. **Help does not operate in a vacuum. There is always an event or occurrence that catalyses help and attracts it. A positive repositioning attracts help to us. This is a reminder to remain actively engaged in the world around you, even when feeling vulnerable and searching for support.**

Esther had to undergo training and preparation in the king's palace for twelve months before she could even qualify to appear before the king for consideration. The training and preparation Esther went through with the eunuchs in the palace positioned her for favour before the king. The parable of her story is reflected in the studies and disciplines of groups around the world. True wisdom in a subject comes from years of commitment to the subject matter. Being well positioned takes years of commitment to the subject matter that comprises your existence. What subject matter is that? The choice is yours, but it is recommended you open your ears to the advice from God and your Helpers of Destiny along the way.

We cannot underestimate the place of the process of training and preparation to qualify us to be connected to our helpers of destiny.

It was indeed in the destiny of Esther to become a Queen, but the uncle of Esther, Mordecai, had to enlist her as one of the candidates for the position to have the opportunity to contest.

Opportunity to fulfil destiny will come when we are well positioned; but we need to recognise such divine opportunities when they come, and take good advantage of them. Certain opportunities can make us for life, so handling your affairs properly is of the highest order of importance.

An important prayer one should pray always is that one does not misuse, abuse or miss any divine opportunity that comes one's way.

Abraham was sitting at the tent door in the heat of the day, probably by noon time when the heat was absolutely oppressive. He lifted up his eyes and saw three men passing by. These men struck a chord with him, and he was convinced that they were no ordinary travellers. These men were God manifested in the flesh, and they had a message for anyone who was well-positioned to listen. Abraham felt instinctively the spiritual glow of these men and welcomed them with open arms, entertaining them and treating them with honour and dignity. These men gave word that God was angry with Sodom and Gomorrah, and their destruction was imminent. In the same breath, they said that Sarah and Abraham would give birth to a son in the next year, a wonderful blessing. Abraham, in this case, was well-positioned to hear God's message and did not hesitate when he felt a godly presence from these three travellers.

The doubt expressed by Sarah did not stop the promise of God from coming to pass. She conceived and bore a son at her old age, according to the word of God spoken. Abraham was well positioned and when the opportunity came along, he took advantage of the opportunity that led to the fulfilment of a destiny that would not only affect him, but billions of souls.

When we position ourselves for help, we must grab the opportunity the Lord brings our way to fulfil what He has said concerning us.

CHAPTER FIVE

NEVER DESPISE YOUR HELPERS OF DESTINY

"Those that despise people will never get the best out of others and themselves."

—Alexis De Tocqueville

Our helper of destiny is never packaged as we expect - God gives us the helper of destiny as He wills, not as we demand. He alone has the prerogative of how we will be connected to our helper of destiny. We need the discernment of the Spirit to spot our helper of destiny. Many have shut their door of fulfilment by treating their helper of destiny with disdain and contempt. We must be careful, especially about devaluing people close to us: our familiarity with them has caused us to overlook or miss the potential help they could be to us. It is almost as if all the baseline cares and comforts we give our loved ones become warped and taken for granted over time, feeding a cycle of care followed by resentment for lack of acknowledgement - all feeding a growing bitterness. I call it the, "CAN ANYTHING GOOD COME OF NAZARETH ATTITUDE". Our familiarity and closeness with a person should not blind our eyes to the fact that God has assigned them to us for help in a particular area of our life. Our familiarity with loved ones and people close in our life must not breed contempt.

The Lord Jesus could not do many mighty works in His place of birth, Nazareth, because they were familiar with Him there.

> *"Is not this the carpenter's son? Is not his mother called Mary? and his brethren, James and Joses, and Simon and Judas? and his sisters, are they not all with us? Whence then hath this man all these things. "*
>
> **—Matthew 13: 55-56 KJV**

Instead of celebrating the gift in Jesus, those around the man despised Him; and He could not do many mighty works in their midst. That which you do not cherish and celebrate will exit your life. What we respect and act on with desire is what we attract over time. A person who we do not deeply respect is virtually impossible to attract. How can you encourage the best out of a loved one who you show primarily contempt for? You are giving them the worldview that even family members hate them; how will they assume the rest of the world treats them?

We close the door of help when we despise the person God has sent to us to help and assist us. Your helper of destiny could be a beggar in the street or even a lunatic!

Speaking to married couples, they should learn to honour each other in small and large ways, showing gratitude for each and every cherished moment in between. The greatest disservice you can do yourself as a married person is to disrespect and despise your partner. If you have a problem or issue, trust your love and bond will see the disagreement be resolved.

Michal despised her husband, David, becoming barren without any children for life. Queen Vashti was removed as the Queen because she despised her husband, and found no meaningful recourse to clear the air of resentment within the relationship. Proverbs 18:22 KJV says, "Whoso findeth a wife findeth a good thing, and obtaineth favour of the Lord." If a wife is a good thing and a favour from God, then it will be foolish of any man to treat his wife with disdain and disrespect; they are gifts according to Biblical Scripture and should be foundationally treated accordingly. We all agree we need favour and good things to fulfil destiny. 1 Peter 3: 7 re-emphasises the importance of the husband honouring the wife so that their prayers will not be hindered. When prayers are hindered, the destiny is hampered.

Consider again the story of Naaman and reflect how he got healed of his leprosy. It was the Hebrew slave girl in his home that advised him to contact a prophet in Israel, who ultimately healed him. If he had despised the advice of the slave girl, he would have died as a leper. Naaman's servants who accompanied him to Prophet Elisha are helpers of destiny, as they persuaded Naaman to obey the instructions of the prophet that led to his healing. Naaman heeded the advice of his subordinates.

Arrogance makes people think highly of themselves and undermine those that could be their helpers of destiny.

Our parents are some of the closest people in our life. Our parents are the gateway through which we came into the world. They are our foundation.

> *"Honour thy father and thy mother as the Lord thy God hath commanded thee, that thy days may be prolonged, and that it may go well with thee, in the Land which the Lord thy God giveth thee."*
>
> **—Deuteronomy 5: 16**

Honouring our parents helps to prolong our life and enables us to prosper. Many times, parents or parental relationships play a major role as our helpers of destiny. When, you are feeling good parenting taking effect, you embrace it and its positive effects on your life's outlook.

In short, the relationship with our parent impacts our life in ways that are so layered and organically formed, they only manifest after years of development. If you dishonour your parents, you are dishonouring your foundation. No building can stand if the foundation is compromised. Great advice - never despise your parents; they are the most fundamental helper of your destiny. If you do not have parents because of a tragedy or extenuating circumstance, seeking out parental or mentoring advice is of the upmost importance. It will remind you how to be the cornerstone of your own family tree.

Appreciation of people that have helped us in our life travels is an indication that we value their help and that we have not taken them for granted. There is nothing that shuts the door of help as much as ingratitude. Appreciation attracts people to us, whereas petulant ingratitude spurs separation

There is this story told by Winston Churchill about a boy who fell off a pier into the ocean. A sailor, not caring for the danger to his life, dived into the stormy water, struggled with the boy, and eventually brought the lad to safety. Two days later, the boy's mother came with him to the same pier, seeking for the sailor who rescued her son. After finding the sailor, the mother asked,

"Are you the one who dived into the water and rescued my son?"

"I did", the sailor replied.

The mother's next response was, **"Well, where is his hat?" (Templeton, 1998)**

This attitude is an indication of how ungrateful some people can be. Was the hat more important than the life of the boy? This parable makes clear how sometimes, we talk right past things of major significance that deserve gratitude. When they are gone, we suddenly feel the weight of their absence, realizing we didn't take the right perspective with the help provided from our Helpers of Destiny.

Relating the story in the Bible of the ten lepers, Jesus healed the ten of them, but only one came back to express gratitude to Jesus. The one that came back was made whole. - Luke 17: 17-19. This man who returned to express gratitude got something extra. An attitude of gratitude opens more doors of blessing. Even if it feels like a simple, small, or insignificant moment, think of how those moments add up over time, and consider how at a subjective level, they may have a surprisingly deep impact on the other individual.

Another attitude that is spiteful to our helper of destiny is a failure to show that we value their time. This lack of awareness plays out when we continually come late for meetings we have with people; we do not turn up for appointments we have made with people and do not care to call up to apologise or re-schedule; we keep people waiting for hours outside the appointment time we have with them.

The value we put on a person's time determines the value we have for them. When we abuse people's time, we are disrespecting and devaluing their person. We cannot attract the person we disrespect and devalue. Nobody wants to transact business or have a serious relationship with a time waster. Value others' time the way you value your own on this planet – a simple golden rule to leave with you.

CHAPTER SIX

YOUR PUSHERS IN LIFE

> *"When you squeeze an orange, you get orange juice because that is what is inside. The very same principle is true about you. When someone squeezes you - puts pressure on you - what comes out is what's inside. And if you do not like what is inside, you can change it, by changing your thoughts."*
>
> —Wayne Dyer

There are some pushers we need in our life if we want to reach our full potential. These people are not going to pamper us, but they will push us and challenge us in ways that are genuinely uncomfortable and unenjoyable as they happen. Their push might sometimes be painful and wholly lacking in any immediate gratification of pleasure. They will drill and squeeze us; they might even make us cry from what they will put us through.

These essential pushers are your coaches, your mentor rivals, critics, and indeed, your enemies.

COACH

The coach teaches specific tasks and patterns of thought to make you better in a skill, field, or particular subject matter. The coach will instil the discipline to accomplish the task and build exercises that help you acquire the requisite skill. To accomplish the task and acquire the skill in question; you may have to give up certain niceties and go through rigorous training. **The instructions of your coach will not always be pleasant, but you need the push of your coach to fulfil your destiny.** Your coach may be your parents, pastor, manager at work, or business coach. A harsh or perfectionist manager may provide great benefit by pushing relentlessly for excellence from you. Done with love behind it, these tactics give students a lifetime of discipline.

I myself used to have a perfectionist manager who picked up on every little mistake I made. At first it did upset me, but later I changed my attitude and, instead, felt provoked to do my work devoid of any mistake, and with a touch of excellence. I discovered that the attitude of my manager provoked me to excellent performance. A good coach will put you on your toes to deliver an excellent output.

MENTOR

A mentor is relationship oriented. A mentor will stretch you and help you realize the potential they saw in you long before your own eyes were open to it. They are concerned about getting the best out of you; they will drill you to manifest your full potential in the world around you. You may sometimes think they do not appreciate your effort, but their concern is to correct everything that is correctable in you. Their focus is on your consistent development. A true mentor will be harsh on you. To get the best out of your mentor, you must be teachable, humble and accountable. Every day you show up, even if you aren't feeling at "full strength"; it is better than not showing up at all, more often than not. **A mentor teaches from experience and helps you to achieve your goals faster by avoiding unnecessary mistakes.** When we read of the relationship that ensued between Elijah and Elisha in the Bible, it can be seen as that of a mentor and mentee. Elisha had to follow Elijah from Gilgal to Bethel to get the double portion of the anointing upon Elijah. Elijah not only discouraged Elisha from following him but treated Elisha harshly. Elisha had focus and refused to be discouraged. One of the quickest ways to achieve greatness and fulfil destiny is to have a mentor in your life.

> *"A mentor is someone who allows you to see the hope inside yourself."*
>
> —Oprah Winfrey.

The job of the mentor is to instil confidence in you and have an '**I can do it attitude',** despite the challenges, encouraging you even when you seem to want to give up on your mission in life.

RIVALS

Your rivals are those who compete against you, and they usually want what you want. They want to occupy the same space and position you are occupying or gunning for, and they want the same power you want to influence events. There are positions that only one person can occupy at a time. Only one person can be the President or Prime Minister of a nation at a time. We do not have two kings reigning in a kingdom. Competition is driven in a large way by survival of the fittest, as it were. If you want it. you need to fight for it. Rivalry is meant to make you work hard to improve yourself, and realize how you can push yourself forward. Rivalry should not provoke jealousy, hate or spite. Your rival must push you to succeed and be better than the version of your yesterday, not make arbitrary comparisons between two completely different individuals.

However, sometimes, you are forced into such positions – as Hannah was by Peninnah in the Bible. Both were wives of Elkanah, but Peninnah ruthlessly mocked Hannah for not bearing any children. The taunting of Peninnah did not break Hannah, but instead drove her to see through the pain of the mocking and keep her prayers to God, not petty vengeance. Driven by the character foil of Peninnah, Hannah produced the child that would one day become a key prophet to the Nation of Israel.

CRITICS

Your critics are those who review and assess you and give you feedback on matters you are concerned with. Your critics may be either destructive or constructive. Be they destructive or constructive, they are undeniably pushers in your life. Destructive criticism hurts in a negative way; but one needs to get past the negativity and extract the part of the criticism that is true to make a change for the better. For instance, you kept a client waiting for you because you came late to the office. In annoyance, your manager scolded you and said, "You never do anything right". The criticism of your manager was spiteful and untrue – you can do plenty of things right – but looking beyond the petty criticism, you knew the lateness was your fault because you woke up late. You could adjust by ensuring that you put your alarm clock on to wake you up early. Though the criticism was harsh, you never allowed it to demoralise you; with the proper perspective, even these nasty comments can be used to correct yourself.

Remember the story of Hannah and Eli the Priest in the Bible. Eli wrongly accused Hannah of being drunk while she was praying. Instead of taking offence at the false accusation, she humbly explained her situation to Eli, who then blessed her and agreed that God will grant her prayers. Hannah's prayer was answered, and she gave birth to a male child as requested. God used the false critic to answer the prayers of Hannah because she had the right attitude to the criticism. She endured it – fair or not – until the truth emerged and her prayers were answered.

Consider the response of Jesus to a Canaanite woman who asked Jesus to help deliver her daughter who was vexed with a demonic spirit. Jesus answered and said,

> *"It is not meet to take the children's bread and cast it to dogs."*
>
> **—Matthew 15:26**

The woman replied,

> *"Truth, Lord: yet dogs eat of the crumbs which fall from their masters' table".*
>
> **—Mathew 15:27**

Jesus practically called the woman a dog. The response of Jesus seems insensitive and offensive, but the woman refused to be offended, and used the insult as a tool of strength.

Jesus impressed by her response said,

> *"O woman, great is thy faith: be it unto thee even as thou wilt."*
>
> **—Matthew 15:28.**

The woman's daughter was delivered because she never took offence at what seemed to be harsh words from Jesus. Our positive response to a harsh and insensitive criticism can work in our favour to help us.

Constructive criticism is not about fault finding but helping us in areas that need rectification. It is meant to have a transformative impact upon our lives. Resistance to constructive criticism is proof of arrogance and a tell-tale sign of insecurity. An arrogant and insecure person can never fulfil their destiny.

Jethro, Moses's father-in law, criticised the way Moses was the only one resolving conflicts. Jethro then advised Moses to delegate the responsibility downward and not assume all the burden. It was a constructive criticism, which Moses took on board and thereby instituted the counsel of Jethro - See Exodus 18: 13-27

> *"Whatever you do in life surround yourself with smart people who will argue with you."*
>
> —John Wooden

ENEMIES

Your enemy is someone you see as an adversary – someone who constantly berates and attacks you in an offensive manner. Most times, we feel we do not have anything to do with our enemy. We often pray that God will frustrate the plans of the enemy and condemn them like He did, Sodom and Gomorrah. The hard truth is that God does not always answer such spiteful prayers. He knows that, ultimately, we need the immediate danger of the enemy to propel us toward our destiny.

The reason being that we need such an attack of the enemy to propel us to the place of our destiny.

> *"Friends create comfort, enemies create change"*
>
> *The difference between significance and insignificance is a worthy adversary*
>
> —Mike Murdock.

Consider a case whereby people plot against you in your office and bring false accusations against you, which leads to dismissal from your job. This will no doubt upset you and cause you pain. Take a step back in these moments of acute pain and loss. God may be using the incident to take you to a higher level of your destiny. It will be your approach and response to the attack of the enemy that will determine whether you are prepared to move to the next level.

We need to come to the point at which we see the enemy not only as an adversary to be destroyed, but a destiny anchor to be respected and dealt with accordingly. Without a battle, there can never be a victory. The challenge of the enemy is allowed to elevate and promote us, with the aim of leading us to our destiny. What the enemy thought would bring you down should be used as a pedestal to climb to the top. The stone that the builder refused will always be the head cornerstone. Heed these words!

That mother, father, brother, sister, uncle, aunt or boss at work who might have abused you, misused or oppressed

you… they have only strengthened you. In fact, they might have taught you a lesson in loving the unlovable.

God uses the hard and painful experiences from our enemies to humble and mould us in preparation for the place of our destiny in life. There are some pains from the enemy God will allow, despite all our prayers and positive confessions. For the will of God to be done and for us to fulfil our destiny in life, God allows the temporary afflictions from the enemy for a season, and good reason.

A story was told of a goat that fell into a deep well and could not get out. To add to the goat's predicament, the well was to be blocked with sand and stone. As sand and stones slowly filled the well, the goat shook them off and stood upon them. As the goat continually shook off the sand and stones, it was elevated to the top until it could climb out of the well. The sand and stones that would have buried the goat in the well became the materials that brought it out.

When we consider the biblical story of Joseph, we find out that his enemies actually became his helpers of destiny. Joseph's brothers sold him into slavery, thinking they had ended his dreamy prophecies. Ironically, it turns out that he was sent to Egypt to fulfil what they thought they had banished. The house of Potiphar was like a comfort zone for Joseph, but Potiphar's wife raised a false accusation against the dream seer of an offence he did not commit, and he ended up incarcerated. By divine arrangement, Joseph needed to be in prison to meet the chief butler to interpret his dream. When it was time for Joseph to manifest his destiny, the chief butler, who Joseph met in prison, recommended Joseph as the one capable of interpreting the dreams of Egypt's Pharaoh.

Joseph was sold into slavery and sent to prison by his enemies. Remarkably, even in these dungeon-like conditions, Joseph was elevated from prison to become the prime minister of Egypt. Joseph did not languish in prison

God used the affliction of the enemy to deliver and promote Joseph to be the second most powerful person in Egypt at the time. He became the most Christ like figure in the Old Testament, one who embraced his brothers even after they cast him off like an unwanted child. Thus, by learning to rise above all criticism, positive and negative, Joseph manifested his destiny as a vital prophet of God.

There was a story of a Christian who rode his bicycle to work every day, and on the way, he would pass the local prison. As he rode past, he had a passion for the prisoners that spurred him to pray in his heart, "Dear Lord, bless the prisoners in this jail. May they hear the good news of Jesus Christ and come to know Him as their saviour". One day as he was going to work on his bicycle, a man in on another bike in front of him ran into a small girl and knocked her down. The man became afraid and rode on quickly. The girl lay in the street, crying with pain, and this Christian man stopped to help and comfort her. A policeman came by at that time and thought the Christian man was the one who had knocked the girl down, so he arrested the Christian man, and took him off to the jail. The man, feeling sorry for himself, prayed "Lord I am innocent. This punishment is not fair. Please get me out of here." It was then he heard a voice within him saying, "Why are you sad? Every day you have been praying for the salvation of these prisoners. Now you are here with them, here is an opportunity to tell them the Good news of Jesus." Though the experience appeared to be painful, God turned the pain into gain by enabling him to give witness to many of the prisoners, leading them to faith in Jesus Christ before he was released from jail. He was quite literally given the chance to give holy lectures and explanation of scripture before being rightfully released. Think of Nelson Mandela when considering these kinds of leaders; Mandela was imprisoned for decades. In the end, he became the "Joseph" of South Africa's national history and heritage.

In a more Biblical example, the Apostle, John, was exiled to the prison Island of Patmos. It was on this Island that he received deep revelation from the Lord Jesus Christ himself. The activity of the enemies served a better purpose of pushing Apostle John to fulfil his destiny.

We always need to thank God for the enemy that has caused us pain. Pain of the enemy is a tool God uses to push us into our destiny. No one said it would be easy.

I agree with the words of wisdom by William Arthur Ward, **"Adversity causes some men to break, others to break records."**

The adversity of the enemy must not break us but make us break records.

CHAPTER SEVEN

BEWARE OF DESTINY KILLERS

> *"Be sober, be vigilant; because your adversary the devil, as a roaring lion, walketh about, seeking whom he may devour."*
>
> —1 Peter 5:8 KJV

"The thief cometh not, but for to steal, and to kill, and to destroy

—John 10:10 KJV."

The thief referred to here is Satan and his agents of chaos. The mission of the devil with his agents is to ensure that people do not accomplish their divine assignment. They employ many strategies to carry out their wicked plot to kill the destiny of those around them, and anyone who gives them the light of day is fair game. Let us explore the tactics the devil and his agents use to derail the destiny of people.

SYCOPHANTS

There is an old fable about the crow and the fox. A fox once saw a crow fly off with a piece of cheese in its beak and settle on a branch of a tree. The fox thought in his mind, "That's for me, as I am a fox," and he walked up to the foot of the tree. "Good day, Mistress Crow," he cried. "How well you are looking today: how glossy your feathers; how bright your eye. I feel sure your voice must surpass that of other birds, just as your figure does; let me hear but one song from you that I may greet you as the Queen of Birds." The Crow lifted up her head and began to caw her best, but the moment she opened her mouth the piece of cheese fell to the ground, only to be snapped up by the fox. "That will do," said the fox. "That was all I wanted." The lesson learnt from this story - beware of sycophants. Sycophants are those who praise you for what they want to get from you. They are flatterers, insincere applauders and bootlickers. They tell you that everything about you is great and excellent, then will slit your throat while still smiling at you. Like the fox, they cause your head to swell to get what is in your hand. They are destiny killers out to enflame your ego and tell you what you want to hear.

> *"And a flattering mouth worketh ruin."*
>
> **—Proverbs 26:28(b)**

A sycophant ruins rather than helps your destiny. They speak good about you for the wrong reasons.

If you surround yourself with sycophants, you are slowly killing your destiny. They will praise you to death, like "yes men" do to businessmen. My senior sister once told me if you laugh hysterically after every conversation with your brother, you are not telling the full truth to each other. If, however, there are frowns afterwards, some bitter truths may have been aired out for everyone's good. Consider the old adage that you should yearn for what you *need* to hear, not what you *want* to hear from those around you. Beware of people that always agree with you on everything. Full agreement does not equate to holding your best interests in mind. Someone can hold a different point of view from you, and not necessarily be antagonistic or rebellious. People with contrary or alternative views might expose the flaws in your position, ultimately helping you to make the right decision. A sycophant around you does not enhance you, but rather they give you a false identity. It is pathetic that there are individuals who prefer praise singers and puppets around them, rather than sincere appraisers and people of integrity.

PARASITES

Parasites are those who cling to you, taking from you and offering you nothing. They are mere receivers and not givers. These are pests. I call them suckers, living on you and milking you till you are dry. They are only after what is in your hand, so to speak. Parasites harvest where they did not sow; they inhabit a place another person has built. A parasite hanging around you will not only waste your destiny, but they will kill it. They are like squatters, who pay nothing for occupying a place in your life. The parasite is with you only for what they gain from you and will never add meaningful value to your life. The only way to deal with parasites is to cut them out of your life. If you are in a relationship, be it love, friendship, business, marriage etc, and you are the only one giving, then that relationship is parasitic. It is advisable that you end such a relationship before it harms your destiny.

Recall the story of Jacob and Laban. Laban manipulated Jacob by marrying off Leah instead of Rachel, deceiving Jacob after seven years of labour to win Rachel's hand in marriage. He then benefitted from Jacob's labour for another seven years. In the final verse Laban is mentioned, it is clear that Jacob has returned from his moment of exile far more powerful than he came, and now Laban asks to form a more formal covenant. Jacob endured and then overcame the parasitical and manipulative nature of Laban to build the Kingdom of Israel.

EVIL COUNSELLORS

King David prayed

> *"Hide me from the secret counsel of the wicked. From the insurrection of the workers of iniquity."*

—**Psalm 64:2**

People will come your way to derail you from your destiny by the kind of counsel they give. You need to remain on your divine assignment, and ensure you carry it out according to God's plan. Any counsel given outside of God's plan must be rejected. Your best counsellor as a Christian is the Holy Spirit. Even when people give you counsel, you need to check it with the Holy Spirit. Many destinies have been killed as a result of evil counsellors, so give heed to what advice you act on.

As an example, The Lord showed the Prophet Ezekiel wicked counsellors in the city:

> *"Then said he unto me, son of man, these are the men that devise mischief, and give wicked counsel in this city."*

—Ezekiel 11:2 KJV

Beware of people that give you evil counsel detrimental to your destiny. You can recall the story in the bible of the young prophet from Judah who went on a divine assignment to prophesy against the altar in Bethel. God instructed the young prophet never to eat and drink in the land. Against the instructions of God, the young prophet yielded to the counsel of the old prophet who met him on his way out of the city. The old prophet deceived the young prophet, saying that God had spoken to him that he should bring the young prophet back to his house to eat and drink. The young prophet was killed on his way back by a lion. His life was cut short, and destiny wasted as

a result of the evil counsel of the old prophet. We should be careful not to take evil counsel that will jeopardise our destiny.
- **1 Kings 13 KJV**

> *"Blessed is the man that walketh not in the counsel of the ungodly,"*
>
> —**Psalm 1: 1(a) KJV**

The psalmist is invariably saying that a person is cursed if they allow evil counsellors to direct their path.

PESSIMISTS

There are some people that hang around you, and their ministry is to discourage you, and tell you that the project you are about to embark upon is an impossibility never to be accomplished. They dampen your spirit when you face the gauntlet of life, and make you feel comfortable in defeat. There, at least they have company. I call them pessimists, fire extinguishers and hope crushers. A pessimist says your dreams can never be accomplished realistically. However, they don't offer a meaningful analysis or explanation of these harsh claims. They simply say them while carrying a negative aura. This aura may neutralise your zeal to fulfil your destiny.

Remember the Biblical story of the spies who went to search the land of Canaan. Ten out of the twelve brought back a negative report, lamenting that there were giants in the land.

They considered the Israelites like grasshoppers before the inhabitants of the land, unable to possess their inheritance. This was most certainly a pessimistic report. The whole congregation, except Caleb and Joshua, allowed this report to make them murmur against God, and question His ability to take them to the promised land. As a result, most of the Hebrews from the age of twenty upward, except Caleb and Joshua, died in the wilderness and never got to the promised land. The pessimistic lack of faith during such trying times led to demise of these individuals in the Bible.

The pessimist questions the ability of a person to fulfil their destiny, aborts the journey towards your promised land, and kills many in the wilderness, ultimately dying after an unfulfilled life. Never surround yourself with pessimists; they are dream, vision and destiny killers.

> *The Pessimist complains about the wind; the optimist expects it to change; the realist adjusts the sails."*
>
> —William A Ward

Pessimists question God's word and prophecy and paint an impossible hypothetical picture to try and invalidate the word of God. We must refrain from giving in to such weaknesses, as illustrated by the Prophet Elisha during a terrible famine in Israel. The lack of food grew so dire that people were killing children for sustenance – an absolute human nightmare. Elisha prophesized in those dire times that an abundance of food would come to the land in the next 24 hours.

A lord who happened to be a close confidant of the King replied that it was impossible, "**even if the Lord would make windows in heaven.**" That was not only an affront to God, but a voice of pessimism. The Prophet did not take the confrontation lightly and said the man will see the abundance as prophesised but will not partake of it, and it came to pass as Elisha prophesised. **See 2 Kings 7 KJV**

DEMONIC CONSULTANTS

It is dangerous for anyone to consult the demonic kingdom for information. Any information obtained from a demonic source ensnares and manipulates people, metamorphizing into a destiny killer. God hates it when people consult demons for help.

A particular King in Israel called Ahaziah went to consult Beelzebub, a demonic god, to find out if he would recover from a disease. The angel of God alerted the Prophet Elijah about it. The king was judged for consulting demonic powers, and he never recovered from his sickness. The life and destiny of the king was punished because of his demonic consultation. **See 2 kings 1. KJV.**

Be careful the stock you put into Zodiac signs; they may lead you astray. Also be wary of asking palm readers, soothsayers, mediums, fortune tellers, sorcerers, enchanters, necromancers, stargazers and diviners for information about your destiny. If you are a practicing Christian, these elements are fuzzy enough that they may lead to darkness, dampening your destiny. The information could be taken as deception, parlour tricks, and sheer emotional manipulation.

In fact, this being a Christian Book, I would say to think of these Zodiac fortune tellers as idols, seemingly harmless, yet potentially demonically orchestrated toward wasteful decision-making. I would advise, just never inquire of these parlour-trick soothsayers, as their information and tactics are full of emotional deception and situational manipulation.

The Apostle Paul was wary of a girl who followed them and cried,

> *"These men are the servants of the most High God, which shew unto us the way of salvation."*
>
> **—Acts 16: 17 KJV**

The girl kept following them and announcing this for many days. Paul grieved in his spirit and knew that the girl, though saying what appeared to be true, was operating by the spirit of divination, and not by the Spirit of God. He rebuked the spirit and cast it out of her.

The Bible says,

> *"There is a way which seemeth right unto a man, but the end thereof are the ways of death."*
>
> **—Proverbs 14: 12 KJV**

What may seem to be factual information from a demonic source is indeed a **poisoned chalice.** Be discerning in the spirit, so as not to ignorantly fall prey to these demonic consultants. These manipulative harbingers of misfortune are not just out in the world, but have also infiltrated the church of God. People who claim to be prophets of God are actually diviners, soothsayers and fortune tellers. Figuratively speaking, it is the signs of the last days when you begin taking the advice of these conspiracy-crazed lunatics.

There are situations where people see or know another person's destiny and want to kill it. Herod was informed about the destiny of Jesus by astrologers who saw the star of Jesus (destiny of Jesus) in the Eastern region. Herod would have killed baby Jesus and terminated his destiny if he was not taken out to Egypt for safety. The petty selfishness of these people almost ended up killing the Saviour himself! People who consult unverified or demonic powers for advice on their destiny will find it severely derailed.

It was for these reasons that God, through Moses, warned the Israelites in **Deuteronomy 18:8-12 NKJV**

When you come into the land which the Lord your God is giving you, you shall not learn to follow the abomination of those nations. There shall not be found among you anyone who makes his son or his daughter pass through the fire, or one who practices witchcraft, or a soothsayer, or one who interprets omens, or a sorcerer, or one who conjures spells, or a medium, or a spiritist, or one who calls up the

dead. For all who do these things are an abomination to the Lord, and because of these abominations the Lord your God drives them out before you."

Demonic consultation is an abomination before God linked backed to false idolatry or the serpent hiding in the walled garden. We should be vigilant and protect our destiny from demonic contamination either knowingly, or ignorantly.

Recall that Balak, seeing the glorious destiny of Israel, employed Balaam to curse them. That was a demonic consultation to kill the destiny of the people of God, but God overturned the plan of Balak. The people of Israel, holy in the lifestyle they lived, made it impossible for Balaam to utter any curse, finding only words of praise for the Hebrew people. Eventually, Balaam even made one of the earliest references to the Messianic Redemption found later in the Bible. Speaking less in tongues and more within the line of Biblical Scripture, Balaam utters:

> *I see it, but not now; I behold it, but not soon. A star has gone forth from Jacob, and a staff will arise from Israel which will crush the princes of Moab and uproot all the sons of **Seth**. **Edom** shall be possessed, and Seir shall become the possession of his enemies, and Israel shall triumph*

—**Numbers 24:17-19**

BLOCKERS

Blockers are people who constitute a stumbling barrier on your journey to your promised land. They frustrate every effort you make to fulfil the purpose of God for your life. Their actions may make you question your divine vision and mission, thinking you are on the wrong path. Blockers suppress us, not allowing people to manifest their God-given potential. Blockers operate as

> *"the Horns that scattered Judah, so no one could lift up his head"*
>
> **—Zechariah 1:21.**

When you are about to accomplish a divine assignment and you encounter a barrier, it is the Blockers in operation:

> *For we do not wrestle against flesh and blood, but against principalities, against powers, against the rulers of the darkness of this age, against spiritual hosts of wickedness in the heavenly places*
>
> **—Ephesians 6: 12, NKJV.**

This verse properly identifies blockers. They are not physical, but spiritual beings in the physical form of principalities, powers, rulers of the age.

Every destiny will be confronted by these blockers, and to overcome them, you need to engage in spiritual self-defence as enumerated in:

> *"Therefore, put on the full armour of God, so that when the day of evil comes, you may be able to stand your ground, and after you have done everything, to stand. Stand firm then, with the belt of truth buckled around your waist, with the breastplate of righteousness in place, and with your feet fitted with the readiness that comes from the gospel of peace. In addition to all this, take up the shield of faith, with which you can extinguish all the flaming arrows of the evil one. Take the helmet of salvation and the sword of the Spirit, which is the word of God."*
>
> *And pray in the Spirit on all occasions with all kinds of prayers and requests. With this in mind, be alert and always keep on praying for all the Lord's people.*

—Ephesians 6: 13-18 NKJV

Fulfilling your destiny does not come on a bed of roses all day and night. There are times you need to fight for it by prevailing over the blockers. This may involve taking some radical and unusual or unexpected steps. The friends of the paralytic man had to take the radical step of removing the roof of the house where Jesus was for the paralytic man to receive his healing. Do not judge these seemingly outlandish motives outright. They may serve a greater purpose not yet seen but ordained by God.

See. Mark 2 :1-5 NKJV

In the parable, the man's friends help overcome the hindrance caused by the crowd. They broke the roof, looking for any means to get Jesus in position to heal the paralytic. In this case, traditional protocols had to be broken in order to overcome potent blockers of divine destiny. Your unpredictability may indeed end up an asset that will mesmerise your destiny blockers.

Blind Bartimaeus stood by the Jericho Road begging for alms and got information that Jesus was passing by with a great crowd. Bartimaeus shouted at the top of his voice, "Jesus son of David have mercy on me." People told him to be quiet, but he cried the more, never allowing the people to silence him. Jesus compelled to stand still as he heard Bartimaeus' non-stop cry for help, attended to him and healed him. His persistence paid off in the face of blockers. We should never allow people to silence us and block us from connecting to our helper of destiny.

See Mark 10:46-52 NKJV

MOCKERS

When mockery is employed against a person, the aim is to discredit everything the person stands for, including their destiny. It trivializes the greater pursuits of their life, making them feel so insignificant as to not be even worth pursuing further. The mocker's goal is to devalue and reduce a person's self-esteem in efforts to make them feel inferior. When being mocked, remember the mocker's goal is to make you lose all sense of self-confidence and hope – don't give them the satisfaction. Show them you don't care that they made fun of what you feel is worth defending. All the mocker does is to undermine your divine assignment and make you take an action detrimental to fulfilling your destiny.

Those who mocked Jesus Christ on the way to Calvary could have succeeded in derailing his divine assignment if he had defended himself from their abuse. Nehemiah's assignment to re-build the wall of Jerusalem would have been frustrated if he had allowed his mockers to undermine his determination and focus. It is natural for you to want to react against the mockers of your divine assignment, but fulfilling your destiny is far more important than wasting your time with the scornful. Self-doubt is normal, even for the most confident among us. Mockers usually lack any self-confidence themselves, so they try bringing those around them down, to feel a dominating sense of gratification.

The folk story of the Man, the Boy, and the Donkey illustrates why mockers of your destiny should be ignored.

A man and his son went with their donkey to market. As they were walking by, a man passed them and said: "You fools, what is a donkey for but to ride upon?" In response to this mocking, the man put the boy on the donkey, and they went on their way. But soon, they passed a group of men, one of whom said: "See that lazy youngster, he lets his father walk while he rides."

The man ordered his boy to get off and got on himself. Having not gone far, they passed two women, one of whom said to the other: "Shame on that lazy lout to let his poor little son trudge along." The man was confused, and then brought his son up with him on the donkey. They moved nearer to the town, and passers-by began to jeer and point at them. The man then stopped to know what they were scoffing at. The people said: "Are you not ashamed of yourself for overloading that poor donkey - you and your hulking son?"

The man and son then got off the donkey to think on what to do. They then decided to cut down a pole, tied the donkey's feet to it, and raised the pole and the donkey to their shoulders. They went along amid the laughter of all who met them till they came to the market bridge, when the donkey, getting one of his feet loose, kicked out and caused the boy to drop his end of the pole. In the struggle, the donkey fell over the bridge, and the forefeet being tied together caused the donkey to be drowned in the river.

There are two lessons to be learnt here:

1. By trying to please the petty criticisms of all, you please none
2. DO NOT allow petty mockers to influence or control your destiny

The donkey died because the old man and boy yielded to the mockery of people. **"Beware of mockers of your destiny, do not let them kill your donkey." In our humble opinion, the boy should have been able to ride the donkey, save for a brief respite for the man. Yes, common sense indeed goes a long way.**

The Religious People

These are champions of religious legalism, using their religious ethics to stifle progress while challenging innovation and creativity. They stand against anything that is not in line with the status quo and oppose anything outside their identified religious comfort zone. They are the Pharisees of this world, creatures of habit who oppose healing on the Sabbath day. They are the people who stay where God was, and not where He is at the moment. Their emphasis is more on what you should avoid doing than the positive things you should do. In general, these extreme kinds of religious zealots are more reactive than proactive. You can spot them because while they may do a great job of riling up their group for condemning certain practices against tradition, they have no good ideas or worthy innovations to offer up themselves. They are fear mongering and holding back individual and societal group progress simultaneously.

ENEMIES WITHIN

"What shall we then say to these things?
If God be for us, who can be against us?"

—Romans 8:31 KJV

There is this saying, "when there is no enemy within, the enemies without cannot hurt you". There is some element of truth to this saying. The enemy within you is more dangerous than the outside enemy. It seems we have the potential to be our own best friend and worst enemy, and the battle within is truly the battle we must all face in life and death. The enemy within can almost seem subconscious even when actively manifesting itself. It operates in secrecy and wields immense power. Make sure you do not discount the enemy within you, and you deal with the threat before it conquers you and hollows out your soul. The enemies within are the most dangerous destiny killers because they feed on the negative traits inherent in you. They know your weaknesses because *they are your weaknesses.*

The negative thoughts that tells you:

- You cannot make it in life
- You will never be wealthy
- You will amount to nothing
- You are a bad parent
- You are not capable of running your home

- You will fail again
- You will not get the contract

They are enemies within you that need to be dealt with. The Bible says as a man thinketh so is he. Your thoughts mould who you become. Your thought patterns could distort or repair who God says you should be.

Unforgiveness, anger, unbelief, bitterness, greed, sexual lust, and other inner weaknesses we have are the enemies within that can derail our destiny.

Moses did not make it to the Promised Land because of his failure to deal with his anger problem, which was the enemy within him. Samson's life was ended prematurely, his destiny killed, because he did not deal with his enemy within: sexual lust.

Many destinies have been aborted by the enemy within that was not conquered. The enemy within us is like a seed that flourishes only in certain neglectful conditions. As a result, we naturally tend not to notice it until the condition for its flourishing occurs, which might be too late because of the havoc it deals on our destiny. It is important that we seriously pray that the Holy Spirit exposes the enemy within us and conquers it before it kills our destiny. Be alert to these naturally forming blind spots. Do not resist them; acknowledge them, heed them, and use the Lord's faith to defend against them.

CHAPTER EIGHT

WHERE DO YOU NEED HELP?

> *The diligent and smart people know life fulfilment hinges on helping others and receiving help at the right time from the right people in the right place.*

Your destiny is not a decision, but a discovery. To discover, we need to explore. It is our responsibility to search and find what our divine assignment is. After discovering our assignment, it should give us a clue as to where we should be seeking help.

When we have discovered where we need the help of others, then it is wisdom to leverage the talents of people around us for individual success and a thriving group dynamic. Our assignment should form the basis of allowing people access to our life. You do not call a medical doctor to come and solve a mechanical problem in an automobile.

Every help we need to fulfil destiny has been placed in the hands of people here on earth. We just have to search with the help of The Holy Spirit and connect to them.

Many have sought help from the wrong person because they have not an understanding of what their real assignment is, or they have not put any plan in place to execute their assignment.

It is a non-starter when we do not know what our assignment is. It is also sad when we do not have any plan in place to implement our assignment. The saying goes "if you fail to plan, you plan to fail". We cannot possibly identify where we need help if we do not have a strategy. A person without a strategy is all over the place and is like a rolling stone that gathers no moss. Let an inner faith allow you exploration of what you want as a strategy for carrying out a meaningful life.

We must always seek for the best person to help us in areas we clearly lack fortitude in. Mediocre aims are ill-equipment to produce bountiful results. We should not shop for the cheapest or most expedient, but the best person. People do not go to the market to purchase average products; they naturally dig for the tastiest and juiciest-looking fruit. Whatever God calls us to do, He wants us to do it with a touch of excellence. It follows that God expects us to engage people who will do an excellent job in areas where we need help.

When God called Moses to lead the people of Israel out of Egypt to the promised land, Moses identified a problem of not being a good communicator. God solved this problem by making Aaron the spokesman of Moses to the people of Israel - Exodus 4:10-14 KJV.

God will always schedule a helper to take care of our apparent disability or weakness that we see as a blockage to the fulfilment of our destiny.

The lame man at the gate of the temple called Beautiful begged for alms from Peter and John as they were about to enter the temple. He was expecting to receive alms from them, but rather they gave him something more meaningful. Peter said:

> *"Silver and gold have I none; but such as I have I give to thee: In the name of Jesus Christ of Nazareth rise up and walk."*

—**Acts 3: 6**

Peter took the lame man by the right hand and lifted him up. His feet gained strength and he began to leap and walk. Such is the miracle of so honestly and earnestly asking for help during a vulnerable moment.

A couple of things here. Initially, this man focused on the wrong object – money. However, the men in front of him solved, not this minor need, but his most pressing problem: restricted movement.

Yet still, the man asks Peter and John for what they cannot give him.

This story paints a picture of how some of us place our focus on the insignificant things at the expense of the significant issues of our life. It begs the question: how do we channel our energies properly to major and minor matters. Furthermore, how do we learn to discern the difference between them?

The story from The Acts of The Apostles also shows how people ask for help from people who do not have what it takes in their area of need. There is a need for us to put our priorities right to access the help we need from the right people. Most people do not know where they actually need help: they have misplaced priorities. We think we want money, but there may be a deeper need wherein money is *not* a direct aim – even if increased wealth is a positive by-product of the aim itself.

Another challenge that arises is the wrong diagnosis of a problem. If we diagnose our problem incorrectly, we end up seeking the wrong solutions and helpers. Imagine this scenario: counsellors at a low-income school are trying to figure out why student grades are dropping. They diagnose it as a problem with student motivation, so they hold seminars about the importance of education, with highly paid professionals coming to give some of them.

Nothing changes in the grades. Why?

The counsellors later find out it was *not a problem of motivation:* the children came from an impoverished part of town that was suffering a food shortage. The children weren't eating breakfast and some, not even lunch. It was not a motivation problem; it was a nourishment problem. After correctly diagnosing the problem, the school found a way to get more meal assistance to underserved students.

CHAPTER NINE

REALITY OF THE HELP OF OTHERS

> *Greatness in live is achieved through teamwork, and not solo work. The great achievers are "The We Did It People", and not "The I Did it People."*

Asking and seeking for help does not undermine your self-worth. We must realise that God will never give an assignment that revolves around us alone. The help of others is part of the process we need to go through to complete the assignment. Our ability to ask and seek help from the right people is a great skill we should be proud of. When people buy into your divine assignment and are willing to contribute their part for it to succeed, you should have a great sense of tremendous accomplishment. Think of how interconnected the world has become over time; we have found more ways to communicate, not less. Let us find ways to gracefully accept all contributions to our divine assignment.

Believe it or not, our success in life is measured by the number of people that buy into our vision and are ready to run with us until the wheels fall off the wagon. It is important that we surround ourselves with the right people who will assist us to achieve our lifelong dreams and visions of destiny. We need supporters like Aaron and Hur that uplift the hands of Moses. We should seek people who are committed to us and will defend our visions and dreams. It is great to have proactive personalities like the three mighty men of David who broke through the troops of Philistines to draw water out of the well of Bethlehem. They left on a mission simply because they heard their King long for a drink of water from the well, and they did not hesitate for a moment 2 Samuel. 23:15-16

If you are starting a business, you need people with the appropriate skills and loyalty, not looters who will wreck your business. For a Church to grow, the Pastor should surround himself with people who believe in the visions God has given unto him, and not fault finders and cynics. Do not marry a woman who does not believe in your vision. As a lady, if you figure that your divine calling does not seem to align with a man's vision, I advise, do not go ahead and marry him unless God instructs you specifically. Find a man with spiritual motives akin to your own personal feelings.

When we open up ourselves to people for help in certain areas of our life, we are acknowledging either our weaknesses or limitations, and submitting our ego: that is powerful. Humbleness is empowering. A complete person is a person who is willing to take from people, and give to people, in the right circumstances. When we accept the help of others, we open the door of fulfilment and become a blessing to those around us.

The idea that we are self-made is an illusion. Whatever be our accomplishment, let us realise that it is a product of the help from people that God has placed in our lives. We play a role in walking through the day but consider all the things that had to go right for you to still be alive, living through your family's generational survival. Our mantra when we achieve anything should be, "We did it", and not "I did it". You have the help of the Holy Spirit alongside you always.

Whatever we are - a CEO of a company, a cleaner, manager, pastor, entrepreneur, employer, employee, or teacher - our fulfilment in life is linked to our ability to work with others to access the right help.

Speaking from a Christian perspective, I need to caution that people who will help us in life do not always come to us naturally as a matter of course. It can seem that the devil puts blockages in our path to hinder us from connecting to the right people around us. To connect to some of our helpers, we have to engage in spiritual warfare in the place of prayer to prevail and take an unusual step of faith.

The woman with the issue of blood in the Bible realised that Jesus was the solution to her problem, but knew that, beyond her prayers, she needed to take some action. She sought for help by touching the hem of Jesus garment and was made whole - Matthew 9: 20- 22. She connected to her helper of destiny by reason of her prayers and the action she took. We should emulate this woman and do likewise.

In conclusion, I would like to share some Holy Ghost inspired prayers that will help you connect to your helpers of destiny. You need to pray this prayer in faith and take the necessary action as directed by the Holy Spirit to connect to your helpers of destiny.

PRAYER POINTS

- Holy Spirit, you are my chief helper, help me conquer every enemy within me.

- The King's heart is in the hand of the Lord, as the rivers of water: he turneth it whithersoever He will, Lord turn the heart of people you have ordained to help me to favour me.

- Lord, let everyone you have assigned to help me, but are bound by the devil, be loosed now in Jesus' name.

- Let every satanic partition between me, and those you have assigned to help me to fulfil my destiny, be removed now in Jesus' name.

- Lord, separate me from every destiny killer around me in Jesus Name.

- Holy Spirit help me to choose the right people to connect to at the right time in the right place

- Ask The Holy Spirit to destroy every ego that will make you despise your helpers of destiny.

- Ask that the Holy Spirit to position you to connect to your helpers of destiny.

- Lord surround me with encouragers and defenders of my destiny

www.ingramcontent.com/pod-product-compliance
Lightning Source LLC
Chambersburg PA
CBHW030043100526
44590CB00011B/318